Life List

poems by

Anne Higgins

Finishing Line Press
Georgetown, Kentucky

Life List

ACKNOWLEDGMENTS

At the Year's Elbow, Mellen Poetry Press: "The Birdwatcher, " "Rain on the
Hedgerows at Higbee Beach," "Tree Swallows, Cape May," "Merlin on the wire,
Bayshore Road"
Scattered Showers in a Clear Sky, PlainView Press: "The Signatures on the
Nests, "Great Blue," "Project Wind-Seine, Cape May," "First Sighting of the
Redstart"
Reconnaissance, Texture Press: "Sometimes a Boy," "Binoculars"

Editor: Christen Kincaid

Cover Art: Sister Marty Dermody, SC

Author Photo: Tina Giaimo

Cover Design: Elizabeth Maines

Printed in the USA on acid-free paper.
Order online: www.finishinglinepress.com
           also available on amazon.com

Author inquiries and mail orders:
Finishing Line Press
P. O. Box 1626
Georgetown, Kentucky 40324
U. S. A.

Table of Contents

I CAUGHT *this morning morning's minion, king-*
  dom of daylight's dauphin, dapple-dawn-drawn Falcon, in his riding
  Of the rolling level underneath him steady air, and striding
High there, how he rung upon the rein of a wimpling wing
In his ecstasy! then off, off forth on swing,
  As a skate's heel sweeps smooth on a bow-bend: the hurl and gliding
Rebuffed the big wind. My heart in hiding
Stirred for a bird,—the achieve of; the mastery of the thing!

  Gerard Manley Hopkins "The Windhover- to Christ our Lord"

Life List:

A cumulative record of bird species that have been positively identified and seen by individual birders. Most birders prefer to record only birds they have observed in natural habitats, and many birders arrange birding tours and travel to local and regional festivals to see more species to add to their life lists.

A list of all the kinds of birds observed by a person during his or her life.

The Birdwatcher

Consumed in the sunshine
of a field full of loss,
riding the gusts of memory,
I call to my sorrows,
elusive warblers
who reply
from the tall grass,
occasional flash of gold,
cedar waxwings
calling from deep
in the green glen.
They're the ones I want to see.
I scorn the more obvious
pigeons and starlings
who scavenge
at my feet.

Count him

Count him among the hummingbirds:
the Violet-Crowned Woodnymph.
His coat electric royal blue,
his neck scarf
iridescent glacier green,
and between his shining eyes,
the crown which names him.
He weighs 2.5 grams.
Imagine leaving your house in the morning
in western Venezuela,
gazing into the foothills,
the humid and wet forests,
and running into him
nuzzling the Heliconia plants
with their redorange paddleshaped leaves,
by your front door.

The Signatures on the Nests

When the trees bare themselves
in November,
the nests emerge.
Clutch the crooks, crotches,
wrists, elbows,
between the fingers,
tangle in the fine hairs
of the topmost branches.

Vacated by their tenants,
the nests cloak their names
in the camouflage of distance.

Nest watchers recognize
the signatures
in salad bowls that perch
on the brink of heavy branches
over the canal
which do not say
robin or cardinal.
Someone else,
larger and more ponderous,
down south now,
owns those.

Saw-whet

Saw it but I was wet behind the ears.
It was wet too, claws whetted for the voles.
Small owl of all types of woodlands,
seven inches long,
roosts in winter in thick pines
in Christmas tree farms,
even in parks and gardens.

Upon discovery it sits quite still,
stares placidly with its large yellow eyes,
unflappable,
but not tame.

I do not hear its
hoarse whistles,
its short, high toots.

Fort Clifton Park, Colonial Heights Virginia

We walked the boardwalk through the little swamp
almost at twilight
almost at closing time
for the nature preserve.
In the quiet,
sudden
flash of buttery yellow
and the Prothonotary Warbler
arrived
three feet in front of us
on a crusty branch,
to feed her flapping fledgling.
Unmindful of us
paralyzed with joy
to see her
so close
so close.

Great Blue

Dawn spread a sheet of satin on the glass
canal and lake and towpath in between.
My walk was interrupted by the scene
of his arrival from the marsh to grass.
I stopped stock still in case he wished to pass,
so I could watch him without being seen .
The wide splayed yellow fingers on the green...
How could such stick straw spindles ever last,
supporting elegance of gray blue girth?
Binoculars allowed him in my reach...
But yellow eyes at last discovered me.
A lift of neck and feather, shrug of mirth,
one blasé glance and off the grainy beach,
into the air of swallowed memory.

Phoebe , nestmaking

Slatey grey on the tilted head,
brown dark shiny eye thoughtful
facing camera
absorbed expression on her face,
fiber filament of last summer bindweed
clutched in beak
ready to add to cushion
the mudspattered floor
on the edge of the ceiling.

Tree Swallows, Cape May

At the meadows
in mid-September, a million silver
tree swallows
wallow and swoop in the air,
taking great swallows of air,
folding up on the tall stalks
of marsh weeds
like shining Christmas ornaments.
As one,
they flash like a flag
of silver and slate blue
against the turbulent blue sky,
unfurling south.

Binoculars

Catering to the desire to see
further than is possible
when using the naked eye,
the desire to see the
Yellow- breasted Chat
who chuckles in the Cape May sun
from a distant treetop,
Binoculars present the opportunity.
Objective lens,
Ocular lens,
Porro Prism
provide precision,
and even better,
eye relief.

Rubber eyepieces now crumble
from age, sweat,
skin oil,
bug spray.
Still the collimation offers
perfect stereoscopic vision.
The interpupillary distance
between the pupils of the eyes
is different for each person.
Thus the central hinge
permits differentiation.

The Yellow-breasted Chat
glows buttery gold
in the sunlight,
appearing eight times closer to me
than he actually is.
I can almost see the lustful glint
in his beady black eyes.

Merlin on the Wire on Bayshore Road

The memory moves faster than the pen.
The merlin lands minutely on the wire,
But flashes off in sunlight as I near.

Behind my eyes are attics full of rooms
whose only access lies in photographs.
The merlin lands minutely on the wire.

That window overlooking maple trees,
where winter sunsets blazed in molten red,
It flashes off in sunlight as I near.

The snowbird that I rescued Easter day
lay stunned but blinking, heating up my hand.
The memory moves faster than the pen.

The morning kitchen silence breaks and hums,
The rubythroat appears, and chirps, and drinks,
he flashes off in sunlight as I near.

The face of one long dead begins to form.
I see his thick brown hair wave in the wind,
He flashes off in sunlight as I near.

The breath of God upon my neck, so clear
and sudden once in one of those close rooms...
The memory moves faster than the pen.

I reach into the ocean's briny mouth.
My hand emerges empty, wet with tears...
The memory moves faster than the pen.

Project Wind Seine, Cape May

Barbara, in the first dim arrival
of the Alzheimer's,
trods clumsily along
beside me
to the naturalist's
station.

He frees the warbler from the net,
weighs it, checks how much fat
protects the tiny body
by blowing on the feathers,
peering at the skin.

Then he hands Barbara
the Magnolia Warbler.
He puts this wonder of wind-caught
gold
caught on its way South,
in her amazed hand.

She holds the bird briefly, then
opens palm,
and it flies on
to its home in
the rainforest.

Rained in at the Jetty Motel, Cape May

Storm drenching the dry coast,
give me your clammy hand!
If I could hear your kiss
on the back of the peregrine,
I would sing until the sky turned green
and laugh like a cricket cough,
but rain's no hesitation.
 Ships wrestle with the message,
the woman at Cape May sits by the window;
the eye knows why she waits inside.

She recalls her last October
in the sacred wood: Yellowrumped Warblers and their cousins,
clicking their fall ticks and busy eating,
fluttered around behind her and above her,
 stopping to look right at her.

October in Cape May is different from September,
and every day is different.
Every night, songbirds rise and fly south.
Every morning, new ones land and settle for the day.
So she goes back, over and over, to see who has arrived.
 She loves to be alone in the silent wood,
 alone except for the busy birds.

Grounded flyer, take your leave.
Carry those nests in your calendar
where each day will remind you that this one
belonged to the robin, this one to the crow.
It's as simple as dust,
as fickle as flies furrowing into the winter.
When we blame the weather, we blame tomorrow.

Breeding Range

Lately I've been swooped by thrashers,
watched and warmed against disasters.
Crowds of robins pull for worms
morning field with waves of gleaners
sparrows patient with their learners
satin parent feathered forms.

Swallows built their nest on light glove
resting on the lip of doormove,
navy satin coats and cream
look down, solemn and alert,
fledglings fed, flutter home unhurt,
more familiar with flight than they seem.

Bluebirds nest in cemetery,
conversation soft and weary,
questing answers as they sing:
We seek homes where light meets lawn,
cavities where tall oak trees yawn.
These we choose above all building.

Rain on the Hedgerows at Higbee Beach

I do desire you, God.
Your touch like rain on my face,
rain on the landscape of my heart,
like a meadow full of weedy
brown late summer grass,
full of field sparrows,
tangled vines full of thorns and berries,
pokeberry, chokecherry, hackberry trees,
full of Cedar Waxwings.
Your rain lingers like dew on that thicket
that is my heart,
that thicket of desires, thorns, thorny questions
and leaf-berry thick hidden places
where the warblers go to eat the purple berries
of my passions, my regrets, my dreams,
fears, imaginings,
a thick, overgrown path, Lord, wet with your rain,
growing and ripening all that fruit for your
Spirit to eat,
Your Spirit in the wings
of a million birds passing through me.

The Chalfonte Survives the Storm Sandy

With the wonders of webcams,
We watch the white building
Backlit by navy skies,
wet macadam glows like satin
on Howard Street
suddenly empty.

Four hours away,
I sit by my laptop
helpless
as anyone right there.

Let this one be the Storm of the Century.
Disasters to the North,
Passover this time.

Driving Back to Spring

From snow still coating the Green Mountains of Vermont,
I drive home from the funeral
through villages at 20 miles per hour
along the side of lakes just thawed along the edges
down to the Welcome to New York sign
South along thruways
across Pennsylvania
where the mountain backs bare brown
and south to Spring—
Daffodils grinning at last.

My first remembered sighting of
my cousin Jack with the wonderful black ink eyes,
Fifties brill creamed pompadour of hair,
sarcasm curling out of his lips as early as eighteen
yet unsarcastically in love
and married young.
Then five children,
two of them touched by God or fate
or the RH factor or a bad smallpox vaccination,
but loved always until and after their deaths.

What is there to say
of what life held for him
back in the days of summer and sarcasm?

First sighting of Andrew Wyeth

Of a rare and famous painter
took place in a bookstore
on Church Street in West Chester.
Andrew Wyeth was browsing
Like an ordinary bird
Like a house wren
When I knew he was
As fine as a fox sparrow.

First Sighting of the Redstart

Coopers Hawk, my password.
With a bang on the window screen,
she pushes off the sill,
snowbird in her talons.

In Wardtown Virginia,
my warbler watch began
with a Redstart
perched on a picket fence
by the country garden
in the May rain.

Spattered in my mother's blood,
I pushed off
into the cold world.

First Sighting of the Winged Sisters

Took place on the boardwalk
in Atlantic City
on April 4 of 1961.
They sailed along, five of them,
white cornettes like sailboats,
their blue grey full skirts billowing.

God's Geese?
No—
God's Mist Nets.

Sometimes a Boy

Sometimes a boy
turns up like a large turnip
in my classroom.

Sometimes he smirks
like a salamander.

Sometimes he gives me
the blank stare
of a mackerel
that tells me
I'm still
the Osprey.

Nearsighted

Although the eye doctor's chart
 melted sadly into the wall ,
I can see this minute before me,
like a snowbird in the feeder
eighteen inches from my face.
We stare at each other through the window.
His black beady eye is watchful.

I also can see nouns and ruins,
 hairs on my arms,
  wrinkles on my hands,
   pulls in my stockings and pills in my sweaters.

I can see the ocean, near me in my mind.
that same bedroom window at Cape May
every summer for 14 summers,
can see it better than the snow squeezing the field.

I can see the hummingbird from five summers ago
better than I can see the finches this morning.
And I can see you, nearby,
on my clothes,
see you with warmth
that lingers.
My glasses
are adjectives;
they clarify,
they make my sight specific
even when they are smudged.

It's Earlier than You Think

It's earlier than you think
when the dark drops down
to detach the retina of the afternoon.
Chickadee the last visitor to the windowsill.

It's earlier than you think
for those brain tumors to flourish
like the last cabbages in the garden.

Earlier than you think
for 25 years to have passed since the Berlin Wall.

Earlier than you think
for my student to turn forty.

Veterans Day, 2014

Kate Smith still sings
God Bless America
at Sunset Beach at Cape May Point, each evening
while flags which draped
the coffins of Veterans
run up the flagpole
and small children
run by the Bayshore.
Too cold to do this in November.
Too dark too early.
One hundred years ago
The Great War began:
young men snagged and dead in barbed wire
like so many sparrows

Sometimes it causes me to tremble

Idly, I wonder:
has a Peregrine Falcon ever landed
in one of the sycamore trees
on Hughes Street
in Cape May City?

Last Good Friday,
stepping out of Peebles Department Store,
I lifted the window struck body
of a Chestnut-sided Warbler still warm
from the pavement.
Took him home.
Buried him in the garden.

Goldfinch dips a scalloped skydance
from my windowsill to the maple tree,
trilling while each day
wings and head and back
turn from olive to lemon yellow.
He's ready for love,
ready for summer,
ready to land on my hand
in my fantasy
of winged things unafraid.

I still ask John Lennon:
What Blackbird sings
in the dead of night?
What Blackbird flies
into the light
of the dark black night?

$\mathbf{A}$nne Higgins teaches English at Mount Saint Mary's University in Emmitsburg Maryland. She is a member of the Daughters of Charity. She is a graduate of Saint Joseph College, Emmitsburg, the Johns Hopkins University, and the Washington Theological Union. She is a native of West Chester, Pennsylvania.

She has had over 100 poems published in *Yankee, Commonweal, Spirituality and Health, The Melic Review, The Centrifugal Eye,* and a variety of small magazines. She has given poetry readings at local bookstores and colleges, and was invited to give a reading at the Art and Soul Conference at Baylor University in February of 2001, and at the Calvin College Festival of Faith and Writing in 2002. Garrison Keillor read her poems "Open-Hearted" and "Cherry Tomatoes" on The Writer's Almanac on October 8, 2001, August 8, 2010, August 12, 2015, respectively.

Five full-length books and three chapbooks of her poetry have been published: *At the Year's Elbow,* Mellen Poetry Press 2000; *Scattered Showers in a Clear Sky,* Plain View Press 2007; chapbooks: *Pick It Up and Read,* Finishing Line Press 2008, *How the Hand Behaves,* Finishing Line Press 2009, *Digging for God,* Wipf and Stock 2010, *Vexed Questions,* Aldrich Press 2013, *Reconnaissance,* Texture Press 2014, and *Life List,* Finishing Line Press, 2016.